NO. CLII.

THE MINOR DRAMA.

THE PERSECUTED DUTCHMAN; OR, THE ORIGINAL JOHN SCHMIDT.

A Farce, in One Act.

BY S. BARRY.

WITH CAST OF CHARACTERS, STAGE BUSINESS, COSTUMES, RELATIVE POSITIONS, &c., &c.

AS PERFORMED AT THE PRINCIPAL AMERICAN THEATRES.

NEW YORK:
SAMUEL FRENCH & SON,
PUBLISHERS,
28 WEST 23D STREET.

LONDON:
SAMUEL FRENCH,
PUBLISHER,
89 STRAND.

SCENERY.

With a view to obviate the great difficulty experienced by Amateurs (particularly in country houses) in obtaining Scenery, &c., to fix in a Drawing Room, and then only by considerable outlay for hire and great damage caused to walls, we have decided to keep a series of Scenes, &c., coloured on strong paper, which can be joined together or pasted on canvas or wood, according to requirement. Full directions, with diagrams shewing exact size of Back Scenes, Borders, and Wings, can be had free on application. The following four scenes each consists of thirty sheets of paper.

GARDEN.

The above is an illustration of this scene. It is kept in two sizes. The small size would extend to 15 feet wide and 8 feet high, and the large size to 20 feet long and 11½ feet high. It is not necessary to have the scene the height of the room, as blue paper to represent sky is usually hung at the top. Small size, with Wings and Border complete, $7.50 ; large size, do., $10.00.

WOOD.

This is similar in style to the above, only a wood scene is introduced in the centre. It is kept in two sizes, as the previous scene, and blue paper can be introduced as before indicated. Small size, with Wings and Borders complete, $7.50 ; large size, do., $10.00.

FOLIAGE.—This is a sheet of paper on which foliage is drawn, which can be repeated and cut in any shape required. Small size, 30 in. by 20 in., 25 cts. per sheet ; large size, 40 in. by 30 in., 35 cts. per sheet.

DRAWING ROOM.

This scene is only kept in the large size, to extend to 20 feet long and 11½ feet high. In the centre is a French window, leading down to the ground, which could be made practicable if required. On the left wing is a fire-place with mirror above, and on the right wing is an oil painting. The whole scene is tastefully ornamented and beautifully coloured, forming a most elegant picture. Should a box scene be required, extra wings can be had, consisting of doors each side, which could be made practicable. Price, with Border and one set of Wings, $10.; with Border and two sets of Wings, to form box scene, $12.50.

COTTAGE INTERIOR.

This is also kept in the large size only. In the centre is a door leading outside. On the left centre is a rustic fireplace, and the right centre is a window. On the wings are painted shelves, &c., to complete the scene. A box scene can be made by purchasing extra wings, as before described, and forming doors on each side. Price, with Border and one set of Wings, $10.00 ; with Border and two sets of Wings, to form box scene, $12.50.

The Drawing Room mounted can be seen at 28 West 23d St., New York. Full directions accompany each Scene.

THE MINOR DRAMA.

The Acting Edition.

No. CLII.

THE

PERSECUTED DUTCHMAN,

OR,

THE ORIGINAL JOHN SCHMIDT.

A Farce, in One Act.

BY S. BARRY,

Author of "A Romance in High Life," "Dick Tarleton," "The Dutchman's Ghost," "Capital Prize," "Who's the Father?" "It runs in the Family," "Tower of London," "Spirit of '76," "Coachman and the Heiress," &c., &c.

TO WHICH ARE ADDED

A Description of the Costume—Cast of the Characters—Entrances and Exits—Relative Positions of the Performers on the Stage, and the whole of the Stage Business.

AS PERFORMED AT

THE PRINCIPAL AMERICAN THEATRES.

NEW YORK:
SAMUEL FRENCH & SON,
PUBLISHERS,
28 WEST 23D STREET.

LONDON:
SAMUEL FRENCH,
PUBLISHER,
89, STRAND.

Cast of the Characters.—[The Persecuted Dutchman

	Original, Bowery, 1854.	*Brougham's Bowery,* 1857.	*National, N. Y.,* 1858.
John Smith or Schmidt, the Persecuted Dutchman, of the Firm of Schmidt, Vondunder, Kelt & Co., N. Y.,	Mr. S. W. Glenn.	Mr. S. Barry.	Mr. S. Barry.
Captain Blowhard, with Blows and Blowing, -	" Byrne.	" D. Whiting.	" C. W. Taylor.
Hon. Augustus Clearstarch, fond of Daughters whose Dads have Dimes. - - - - - - - -	" S. Barry.	" G. E. Aiken.	" L. H. Everitt.
Charles Soberly, a Nice Young Man, particularly fond of Miss Arabella, - - - - - -	" O. Collins.	" F. Hodges.	" H. W. Chapman.
Mr. Plentiful, fond of Customers. - - - - -	" Reed.	———	" S. Bradshaw.
Teddy, fond of Perquisites, - - - -	" Lamb.	" W. Denham.	" G. A. Beane.
Miss Arabella Blowhard, fond of Whiskers and Moustachios, - - - - - - - - -	Miss C. Hiffert.	Miss F. Denham.	Miss Furguson.
Mrs. Plentiful, fond of *Change*, - - - - -	Mrs. Dunn.	Mrs. Axtell.	Mrs. J. J. Bradshaw.
Perseverance, fond of Everything that's Good, -	Miss Wells.	Miss Clifton.	Miss L. Lewis.

Time of Representation, Fifty Minutes

THE PERSECUTED DUTCHMAN.

SCENE I.—*A Room in Mr. Plentiful's Hotel. Table, chair, &c.* L.

Enter MRS. PLENTIFUL, R. 1 E.

Mrs. P. Bless me! here comes the coach, and no one to see to the travelers! Teddy! Teddy!

Teddy. [*Without.*] Here I am, ma'am.

Mrs. P. Why, you lazy Irish bog-trotter! You are there, when you should be here! Teddy! Teddy! I say!

Teddy [*Without.*] Coming, ma'am!

Mrs. P. Well, why don't you make haste? The coach is at the door!

Enter TEDDY, L. 1 E.

Teddy. Here I am, ma'am. Y—a—w! [*Yawning.*

Mrs. P. You lazy fellow! Why don't you go and look after the passengers?

Teddy. Yes, ma'am.

Mrs. P. Are you going? Look, sir; the travelers are getting out Quick, see to their baggage!

Teddy. Yes, ma'am.

Mrs. P. Go along, then! [*Pushes him towards door,* 2 E. L.

At the same time, enter HON. AUGUSTUS CLEARSTARCH, *with* MISS ARABELLA. TEDDY *runs against the* HON. AUGUSTUS.

Aug. You Iwish scoundwel! what the devil are you 'bout?

Teddy. I beg your pardon, ma'am, [*to* ARABELLA,] but my parquisites occupied the edicational part of my sight and parpindicular.

Mrs. P. [*Calling.*] Here, Perseverance! Teddy!

Enter PERSEVERANCE, PLENTIFUL, *&c.*

See to the gentleman's and lady's baggage.

[PERSEVERANCE *takes lady's hat-box, and exit,* R.

Plen. Ah! travelers by the coach, I perceive. You are welcome.

Aug. I say, landlord, your woads are uncommon dusty.

Mrs. P. Perhaps the lady would choose some refreshment before she retires?

Aug. Arabella, love, what say you, dear?

Ara. No, thank'ee, Gussy dear.

Mrs. P. If the lady will step with me, I will show her an apartment.

Ara. Yes, thank'ee; I am very much fatigued.

Aug. In the meantime, I should like to say a word to the landlord.

Ara. Gussy dear, don't stay from me long.

Aug. No, dear. Landlady, bring me a bottle of your best wine. [*Exit* MRS. PLENTIFUL, *with* ARABELLA, *who kisses her hand to the* HON. AUGUSTUS, *who returns it.*] I shan't be long, dear. By the bye landlord, have you change for a fifty dollar bill? It is the smallest I have 'bout me at present.

Plen. No, sir, I have not; but I will endeavor to procure it for you.

Aug. Thank you; you will oblige me vastly. [*Exit* PLENTIFUL, R. 1 E.] Well, 'pon my soul, I hope he will get the change for my bad fifty dollar bill. I have gone to a great deal of trouble to make love to a boarding-school miss. However, her old dad, Captain Blowhard, has a cool fifty thousand; and when I marry Miss Arabella, the old 'un's tin will repay me for all my trouble.

Enter MRS. PLENTIFUL, *with wine—sets it on table*, L. H.

Mrs. P. Your wine, sir.

Aug. Thank you. By the bye, landlady, I wish you would order me an extra coach, as I have business in New York, and wish to reach there to-morrow morning.

Mrs. P. The regular stage *leaves* to-morrow morning at nine o'clock. For an extra one, I shall have to speak to my husband.

Aug. Never mind; you need not trouble your excellent husband. I am very well satisfied with this comfortable hotel and the lady-like deportment of the charming hostess.

Mrs. P. Oh, sir! you flatter.

Aug. Where there is truth there is no flattery. By the bye, landlady, your excellent husband could not procure the change for my fifty dollar bill. I should be eternally obliged to you if you would let me have, say ten or fifteen dollars, till I reach New York, and my fifty dollar bill you can retain as security.

Mrs. P. I should be most happy to oblige you, but I have not the money about me. Perhaps my husband——

Aug. Oh, never mind; I'll not trouble him. You can order the extra stage, and say nothing about it.

Mrs. P. I beg your pardon, sir; but an extra stage is ten dollars more.

Aug. [*Aside.*] Oh, the devil! a pretty business I've made of it! This comes of running away with a boarding-school miss. However, the fifty thousand will pay me for all. I have one good ten dollar note, and I must have the coach; so here goes. [*Aloud.*] Landlady, here is the ten dollars. [*Gives money. Aside.*] There goes the last ten dollars I have in the world!

Mrs. P. Oh, thank you, sir!

Aug. Not a word, madam. And at the same time, allow me to observe, I shall never patronise so mean and contemptible a place again.

Mrs. P. What! not patronise so comfortable a hotel! Besides, the lady-like deportment of the charming hostess! Ha! ha! ha!

[*Exit* MRS. PLENTIFUL, R.

Aug. Confound the impudence of that woman! She takes the last ten dollars I have in the world, and defends herself with my false flattery. Never mind; I dare say Miss Arabella has some money about her. I forgot to question her as regards the extent of funds in her exchequer. Ah! here she comes. I shall soon know all.

Enter ARABELLA, R. 1 E

Ara. Why, Gussy dear, what has kept you so long? Why, what's the matter? Are you not well? Never mind, Gussy dear; we will be much happier when we are married. Won't we, Gussy dear?

Aug. Yes, dear, when we reach New York. Arabella dear, that landlord and landlady are very low people. They wouldn't change my fifty dollar bill, but took all the change I had. I only wanted a little to give the servants. Arabella dear, have you any change about you?

Ara. Why, Gussy dear, papa never permits me to have money; and says, unless I marry cousin Soberly, not a shilling of his money shall I have.

Aug. [*Aside.*] Oh! the devil!! I find I have done very wrong in enticing this young lady from school. Oh, yes; she should go back, by all means.

Ara. Why, Gussy dear, are you not well? You have plenty of money, you know, and it's so much better marrying for love.

Aug. [*Aside.*] Is it, though?

Ara. Come, Gussy dear, let us marry for love. [*Taking his arm*

Aug. [*Withdrawing.*] Miss Blowhard, I find I have done you and your excellent papa much wrong in taking you from school, and the best thing you can do is to return—it is, indeed, 'pon my honor.

Ara. Why, Gussy dear, won't we get married, after all?

Aug. No, I think not. I thought some person would share your papa's money, other than cousin Soberly.

Ara. Gussy dear, won't you marry me?

Aug. 'Twould be doing great injustice to your papa and yourself. You see, my dear, I would if I could; but I can't.

Ara. But you shall, though! [*Crying.*] Oh! oh! oh!

Aug. Don't cry, my dear; it's highly improper.

Ara. Why, you ugly, horrid, villanous, cat-faced monkey!

[*Drives him into corner*, L.

Aug. Now, my dear, take my advice and go back to school.

Ara. I'll tear your eyes out!

Capt. [*Without.*] Never mind, I'll find him.

Aug. Hallo, the Captain's voice. You had better take my adv[illegible] and go to your papa.

Ara. But I won't, though. I won't marry cousin Soberly, I'm determined. Boo! [*Exit*, R. 1 E.

[HON. AUGUSTUS *goes up to table, seats himself and drinks. Enter* CAPTAIN BLOWHARD, L. 2 E.

Capt. Ah! the scoundrel! the landshark! to rob me of my dear little Arabella; Only let me come across him, and damn me, I'll—— [*Sees* HON. AUGUSTUS *at table.*] Hallo! who have we here? Perhaps this is the rascal. I say, sir!

Aug. [*Aside.*] Now for a little impudence.

Capt. I say, sir!

Aug. Ah! my dear sir, did you remark?

Capt. Yes, sir! I am here in search of the scoundrel who ran away with my daughter

Aug. Your daughter! Why, you haven't a daughter, have you? I congratulate you! [*Takes* CAPTAIN'S *hand.*

Capt. [*Snatching it away.*] No, sir! yes, sir! damn me, sir! And if I'm not mistaken, you are the rascally seducer!

Aug. My dear and respected old gentleman, you do not suppose for a moment that I am the person who robbed you of your child. No, sir. Now I remember, a person came to this house with your daughter, and, hearing you were in pursuit of him, he left immediately; and leaving your daughter without a protector, I volunteered to accompany her to her home, and see her safely in her respected father's arms.

Capt. You did, did you? Why, you damned, good-natured, noble-hearted, gentlemanly, whole-souled fellow, give me your hand. Ha! ha! ha! that I should suppose for a moment that you——

Aug. [*Aside.*] Should be the very man! [*Aloud.*] Ridiculous—ha! ha!

Capt. Well, you remember the old saying, "Mistakes in the best-regulated families." I ask your pardon, sir. My name is Blowhard, and any service I can render you, you have only to name it.

Aug. Now I think of it, it may be in your power to oblige me. The fact is, when I arrived here, I expected to find a remittance. Unfortunately, as yet, it has not come to hand. If you will let me have the small sum of fifty dollars till I arrive in New York, I shall be eternally grateful.

Capt. Fifty dollars! with pleasure. Yes, sir, a hundred if you want it.

Aug. [*Aside.*] My luck! I should have made it a hundred.

Capt. By the bye, Mr. ——ah! I beg your pardon—what is your name?

Aug. Sir, did you speak? Oh! my name. [*Aside.*] What the devil is my name? [*Aloud.*] Brown—Theophilus Brown.

Capt. Well, then, Mr. Brown, I have not a fifty, but here's a hundred; I hope it will do as well.

Aug. Thank you.

Capt. Not a word. And now, Mr. Brown, I should like to have you tea with me this evening.

Aug. With pleasure. What time?

Capt. Seven o'clock. Ha! ha! ha! I can't help thinking of the scoundrel. As soon as he heard of me he left, did he? and you rescued her! ha! ha! ha!

Aug. Capital joke—ha! ha! [*Poking him.*

Capt. Sh—h! ha! ha! ha! [*Seriously.*] If I could lay my hand on the scoundrel, [*places his hand on* HON. AUGUSTUS,] I'd blow his brains out.

Aug. You'd blow his brains out, would you? ha! ha! ha! Well, Captain, I hope you'll excuse me; I have business, and——

Capt. I say, Brown—remember, seven o'clock.

Aug. [*Aside.*] I will be seventeen miles away. [*Aloud.*] I'll not forget. I say, Captain, a capital joke, wasn't it? ha! ha! ha! Good bye. [*Aside.*] Damned old fool! [*Exit*, R. 1 E.

Capt. Ah! that's a glorious chap! Now for my daughter.

Enter TEDDY, R.

Teddy. If you plase, sir, there's a lady in the parlor that would spake wid ye.

Capt. I'll be there in a moment.

Teddy. All right. I'll tell the lady, after a while. [*Exit*, L.

Capt. That's her. And for that scoundrel, I'll give as much as I gave my friend Brown to lay eyes upon him. And Arabella—if she refuses to marry her cousin Soberly, I'll cut her off without a dollar. [*Exit*, R.

Schmidt. [*Without*, L. H.] Gone away! What you do?

Teddy. [*Without*, L. H.] Well, sir, I want my parquisites.

Enter SCHMIDT, *followed by* TEDDY.

Schmidt. Gone te duyvel mit yourself.

Teddy. What might your name be, sir?

Schmidt. I am John Schmidt.

Teddy. I thought John Smith was dead.

Schmidt. No, humbug! I am te original John Schmidt.

Teddy. Well, Mr. Smith, I want my parquisites. [*Goes to take carpet-bag.*

Schmidt. You can't steal mine garpet-bags.

Teddy. Ye's *lying*—under a mistake.

Schmidt. You tell me I'm lie, I vill blow your nose off. [*Squares himself—puts down carpet-bag—*TEDDY *takes it up.* SCHMIDT *scuffles with him.* TEDDY *trips him—he falls on stage with carpet-bag in his arms.*] Oh, mine bump! If mine vrow have seen you drip up mine heels von top tis floor, un bang mine bump, she would give you te devil. I will have te constobber to take you mit te bost-office. [TEDDY *helps him up.*

Teddy. I hope you're not hurt, sir. You're mistaken; I'm the servant. [*Brushes him off.*] I beg your pardon, sir.

Schmidt. You begs mine bardon. Vell, I don't care Der ish mine hand. I am John Schmidt, von ter firm of Schmidt, Vondunder, Kelt un Co., boot un shoes tread fnters, un nunder tinks.

Teddy. I'm here, sir, waiting yer orders. What'll ye have, Mr. John Smith?

Schmidt. I van some larger pier un spretsel—von leetle glass dat ish not as much as tri cent.

Teddy. A little glass, Mr. Smith! You have mouth enough to swallow a hogshead. [*Exit* TEDDY, R.

Schmidt. Dat ish funny fellow. He drips up mine heels, un den he pegs mine bardon; un ven I ask him for tri cent glass larger bier, he say mine mouth is pig as hogshead mouth. Ven I vash leetle poy, as no pigger ash dat, ter gals say tat mine mouth ish burty, un mine frow say tat mine mouth ish burty, un by dinks I dink so, too.

Enter MRS. PLENTIFUL, *with beer.*

Mrs. P. Your beer, sir.

Schmidt. Vot vilst too haben vor tat?

Mrs. P. Three cents, sir.

Schmidt. Yaw! Ter ish five cent—I vill haben two cent change.

Mrs. P. Very well, sir; I will send the change.

Schmidt. Landlady, have you got von leetle bit onion tat ish notinks tat you will give to me mitout any charges?

Mrs. P. Well, that certainly is meanness. I'll see, sir, and send the change by Perseverance.

Schmidt. Landlady, I have gone to sleepen dill ter-morrow morning. Vot you ask for un bed?

Mrs. P. Fifty cents.

Schmidt. Fifty cent! my Got un hemmel! Why, I gets un bed in Chatham Street, New York, for swelve un a half cent.

Mrs. P. You will remember, sir, you are not in New York; and if you obtain a bed here, fifty cents will be the charge.

Schmidt. Landlady, I don't mean ter bed; I only vant sometinks to lay down mit, un shut mine eyes open—sometinks dat cost not ash moch ash fifty cent.

Mrs. P. There is a room next to my own, which is not occupied, you can have for fifty cents. I'll send your change immediately.

Schmidt. Landlady—two cent change.

Mrs. P. I remember—*two cents.* That is the meanest man I ever saw. [*Exit*, R.

Schmidt. Fifty cent for von ped! Tat ish enough to set up von saving bank, un many saving bank hash got not ash moch as dat.

Enter PERSEVERANCE, *with onion.*

Per. Here is your onion.

Schmidt. Tat ish nice leetle gal. I have got un boy tat ish un gal she ish 'pout your age, if she ish older ash you.

Per. Why, sir, I am not a *little* girl—I am nineteen.

Schmidt. Never mind; you are nice, good gal, un wen I goes away, I will make you un present.

Per. Make *me* a present, sir?—what?

Schmidt. Yaw—of a kiss

Per. Thank you, sir; we ask double for that.

Schmidt. Well, I won't take some. [*Goes up*

Per. He's a brute, and has no taste for luxuries. [*Exit*, R. 1 E.

Schmidt. [*At table.*] Tat was a burty leetle gal, un if she hadn't charges so moch, I would make her von present mit a kiss before I go. Tis onion ish ash strong dat if you but him on top tis table for five minute, he jumps all round so moch ash like ter spirit-knockers. [*Drinking beer.*] Damn dat! Dis ish nix larger—dis good for nix. Never mind, I drink him—I have paid tri cent for him, and I will drink him for revenge. [*Brings chair down, sits* C.—*business with onion.*] Now I will see what John Schmidt, von ter firm of Schmidt, Vondunder, Kelt un Co., have done mit his collector tour. Tis ish mine accounter book. [*Takes out book.*] I have but down ter customers who have bought shoe thread un nunder tinks von ter firm of Schmidt, Vondunder, Kelt un Co. Ter ish John Schmidt—he can't pay his bill because he have got no money. Dat ish ter lie. Johannes Von Skelter—he can't pay his bill because his frow ish tead. I guess I get him when he get anunder von. Christopher Koons—he can't pay his bill because his frow ish not tead. I get paid dat when she kick von large bucket. Peter Funk—he can't pay his bill dill he get a new stock. By tam, dat will never be. Peter Funk is a tam rascal. Honnes Von Hop-un-nof-fes-hung-gel-es-sen-hel-stum-kim-mell-pons can't pay his bill because he have gone to California Dat ish good for nix. To save five tollar a week, what I have pay mine clerk un I discharge, I have come on tish collector tour, un by dinks, mine expense have been much more ash I have collect. Never mind; I will have un good night's sleepen, un den I will go to Nie Yorick. I will never collect mit mineself again. After I fine dat John Schmidt have no money, (dat ish not me,) un Von Skelter frow ish tead, un Christopher Koon's frow ish not tead, un Peter Funk has got no new stock, un Honnes Von Hop-un-nof-hung-gel-hel-stum-kim-mel-pons has gone to California—no, by dinks, I will never been a collector. Now, good night, un I will gone to sleepen. [*Exit*, L. 1 E

SCENE II.—*A Room in Mrs. Plentiful's Hotel.*

Enter SOBERLY *and* ARABELLA, R. 1 E.

Sob. At least, Miss Blowhard, you should be happy in being rescued from a villain.

Ara. To be sure, cousin Soberly, I am very grateful; but he was handsome.

Sob. Now, my dear Arabella——

Ara. And such a pair of moustachios——

Sob. Be quiet, now do.

Ara. And those darling whiskers——

Sob. No more, Arabella. He was a villain. He thought only of your money. I love you for yourself alone. Name the happy day that will make you mine forever.

Ara. Cousin Soberly, how would I look as Mrs. Soberly, and the mother of a lot of little Soberlys?

Enter CAPTAIN BLOWHARD, L.

Capt. Soberly, everything is prepared; and before long, these quarters will be too hot to hold the scoundrel. I will let him know that I am not to be insulted with impunity. First, I tea with your protector, Mr. Brown.

Ara Papa, to whom do you allude ?

Capt. Mr. Brown, the gentleman with the moustaches, and [*describes coat*,] who rescued you from that villain.

Ara. La, papa ! that's not Mr. Brown. That is the Hon. Augustus Clearstarch, and those dear moustaches that charmed me so !

Capt. The scoundrel ! Why, I have asked him to tea, and loaned him a hundred dollars, beside.

Soberly. Did you loan your money to a perfect stranger ?

Capt. Yes, sir ! Well, sir ! what is it to you, sir ? Damn me ! Here, landlady !

Enter MRS. PLENTIFUL, R.

Landlady, who is that rascally scoundrel with the moustaches and fur coat ?

Mrs. P. I do not know, more than that he came here with this young lady, and has taken a room for the night. He endeavored to borrow fifteen dollars from me, but I wasn't fool enough to lend it.

Capt. But I was, though. Have you a good stout horse-whip ?

Mrs. P. Yes, sir. [*Goes to wing and gets whip—gives it to* CAPTAIN.] There, sir.

Capt. This shall draw from him the satisfaction I require. For you, Soberly, load your pistols to the muzzle—call him out—shoot the rascal !

Soberly. I'll blow his brains out, Captain.

Ara. That's right, cousin Soberly, shoot him right through the gizzard.

Capt. Landlady, show me the room. *I'll* draw from him a confession, and *you*, Soberly, blow him to the devil ! [*Exeunt*, R.

SCENE III.—*A Chamber in 4th Grooves Door*, R. 2 E.—*bed*, C.—*fire-place*, R. 3 E.—*window*, L. U. E. *Table, lighted candle*, L. *of bed—chair—slippers under bed—boot-jack under table—large hogshead above fire-place—tormentor doors closed.*

Enter SCHMIDT, L., *with carpet-bag.*

Schmidt. Aha ! Dere, by dinks, dis ish von goot room, un der ish some bed, vot nobody have gone to sleepen mit. Now, dis ish nice—better ash any bed dat I have layed down on top of myself. Now I will dake off mine boots von top mine feet. [*Takes of boots, whistling*

Enter TEDDY, *singing* "St. Patrick was a gentleman"—*takes* SCHMIDT'S *boots, and is going off.*

Hallo, you Irishman ! vot you do mit mine boots ?

Teddy. You want your boots blacked, and I want my perquisites

Schmidt. If you don't put down mine boots down, I will blow out your prains out mit dis poot-jack.

Teddy. Bedad, I'm not to be robbed of my parquisites, Mr. Smith; nd on the payment of six and a quarters cents in the morning, you an have your boots.

Schmidt. You devil Irishman! You steal mine poots un I will put you on top ter Tombs ven I come to Nie Yoricke. Come back, you Irishman.

Teddy. Nix cum a rouse! Are you Smith, the blacksmith? Nix cum a rouse in a Dutchman's house. This will do for my parquisites, Mr. John Schmidt. [*Exit with boots,* L. 1 E.

Schmidt. Nix cum a rouse in a Dutchman's house! Devil Irishman! Mr. Schmidt have lost his wig un save his bacon. He have gone. Never mine; I can get mine boots when daylight has come. Nix cum a rouse! I will like mine frow to catch him, un give him somedinks what she give me sometimes. Now I will prepare vor mine sleepen. [*Gets cap out of carpet-bag, takes off coat and waistcout, hangs them on chair—puts on cap—takes candle—looks under bed.*] I will be sure ter ish no thieves. [*Takes pillow off—shakes and examines it.*] I don't want some company in bed mit me but mine frow. [*Replaces pillow.*] Dat ish all right. [*Gets in bed.*] Dere, dat ish better pefore ash pehind. Now I will shut up mine eyes wide open tight, and snore away as I please.

Enter MRS. PLENTIFUL, L. H.

Mrs. P. Well, I declare! if that Dutchman hasn't taken this room, and bless me! he's in bed with his boots on! Sir! Mister! you good for nothing fellow! get up!

Schmidt. [*Sits up in bed.*] Landlady, you gone away! Dis ish a single bed. [*Lays down.*

Mrs. P. Single or double, you don't lie in it without paying me fifty cents. And another thing, you monster, you're in bed with your boots on.

Schmidt. Nein, I have not mine boots on.

Mrs. P. I say you have, sir.

Schmidt. Look dere! [*Pulls up clothes—shows feet.*] Ish ter some poots dere?

Mrs. P. Now, sir, pay me for the bed.

Schmidt. I will, to-morrow, mine goot vomans.

Mrs. P. No you don't, sir. You want to get off without paying. I'll take these [*taking coat, &c.*] till I am paid. So, good night, sir. [*Takes candle.*

Schmidt. Landlady, I want to go to Nie Yoricke to-morrows, un I have no clothes. [*Feels pocket for money.*] Stop, I get mine money. Some thief has steal my pocket-book!

Mrs. P. I know you, sir, and it won't do. So good night.

Schmidt. Landlady, leave the candle.

Mrs. P. No, sir.

Schmidt. Landlady!

Mrs. P. Well, sir?

Schmidt. Don't you forgot dat two cents change.

Mrs. P. Good night, Mr. Confidence.

[*Takes candle and exit*, L. 1 E. *Stage dark.*

Schmidt. She have confidence to steal mine clothes. Mrs. Schmidt Mrs. Schmidt! if you could see your poor John, she not cry von bit she would laugh at me. Un if dis old woman kill me, she would dance top von mine grave. Dere ish mine pocket-book, dat is stole away; mine nice pran new second-hand coat, vot I have pought un Chatham Street, Nie Yoricke, for two tollars—tat ish gone; my waistcoat jacket, un all mine tings! I am un bad luck Dutchman! I will go sleepen. [*Lies down.*

Enter AUGUSTUS, *with white gown and long paper hat*, R. 2 E.

Aug. I can't be mistaken. This must be the landlord's room. Now for that ten dollars I gave his wife this morning. [SCHMIDT *snores.*] Yes, that is his hearty snore. Ah! here is the bed. Landlord!

Schmidt. Sh—scat!

Aug. Landlord, I want you.

Schmidt. [*Raises head.*] Mine Cot un Hemmel! dat's de devil!

Aug. Landlord, no trifling. Hand over that ten dollars I gave your wife this morning.

Schmidt. I have not ten dollars. I am somebody else. I am not mineself. Where you come from?

Aug. I came from below, and I have been pretty well roasted down there.

Schmidt. By dinks, it is him! Why don't you stay home, Mr. Devil? I don't live in dis douse. I am ter original John Schmidt.

Capt. [*Without.*] Never mind, I know the room.

Aug. Ah! the Captain's voice! I'll meet you again, sir, and I'll have my ten dollars, you villainous swindler! [*Exit*, D. 2 E. R.

Schmidt. [*Sitting up in bed.*] Swindler! Who tid I ever swindle? He's mistaken, I am somepody else.

Enter CAPTAIN BLOWHARD, D. 1 E. L., *with candle, which is suddenly put out as he enters.*

Capt. I need no light to punish a scoundrel. [*Comes up and strikes bed with whip*—SCHMIDT *jumps up.*] So, sir, I've found you—you rascally seducer!

Schmidt. You are mistaken. I am somebody else.

Capt. I *know* you are Mr. Brown, and that's sufficient.

Schmidt. I am not Brown, I am te original John Schmidt.

Capt. Brown, or Smith, did you not decoy Arabella from her father's arms.

Schmidt. Nien.

Capt. Did you not seduce my child?

Schmidt. Nien, I never induce nobody.

Capt. Did you not swindle me of a hundred dollars?

Schmidt. Nien.

Capt. Are you not a liar?

Schmidt. Nien! I never lie but in my bed.

Capt. Is not your name Brown?

Schmidt. I dell you I am de original John Schmidt.

Capt. I'll make you confess you are a seducer, a liar, a swindler, a lian, and that your name is Brown.

Schmidt. Mine Cot in Hemmel! vot a peoples!

Capt. Now, sir, [*beats him*], are you not a seducer?

Schmidt. Nien. [CAPT. *beats him*]. Yaw! yaw!

Capt. Are you not a swindler? [*Beats him.*

Schmidt. Nien! I am no swindler. [CAPT. *beats him.*

Capt. You are not? [*Beats him.*

Schmidt. My Cot in Hemmel, yaw, I am a swindler.

Capt. So much, so good

Schmidt. So much, tam pad.

Capt. Are you not a liar and a villain.

Schmidt. Nien. [CAPT. *beats him*]. Yaw, yaw, I am a Dutch villain, John Schmidt.

Capt. No, sir, your name is Brown. Are you not Brown?

Schmidt. Nien. [CAPT. *beats him.*] Yaw, yaw, I am black and blue.

Capt. I am satisfied for the present, but I shall send another injured party to you. So good night, and pleasant dreams, Mr. Brown. [*Exit*, L.

Schmidt. [*Sitting up in bed, crying.*] Oh! oh! oh!—Boo! oo—oo—oo! I shall die, I shall be killed in dis house. Oh, my poor frow! She will never see her husband, John Schmidt, not any no more.—What will become of me!

Soberly. [*Without.*] I'll find him, Captain.

Schmidt. Te tuyvel! dere is un under one! He shan't find John Schmidt. [*Jumps out of bed, falls over chair, feels for bed, finds carpet-bag, goes up to window.*] Here is von window, now I will jump out. [*Carpet-bag drops out of his hand. Crash without.*] Dere goes mine carpet-bag, now I will jump out. [*Dog barks.*] Now I will *not* jump out. I will go to bed. [*Gets into bed, head to audience.*] They shall find mine feet un not mine head.

Enter SOBERLY, L.

Soberly. So, this is the room described by the Captain. Here is the bed. [*Shakes Schmidt's feet.*] Sir, sir.

Schmidt. Vot you want?

Soberly. I come to demand the satisfaction due a gentleman.

Schmidt. [*Sits up.*] Now, Mr., what have I done?

Soberly. You have plucked the bud of love from the fair branch, and left it to wither and decay.

Schmidt. This is a poet-robber. I don't know sometinks 'bout dat, Mr. Robber.

Soberly. Come, sir, follow me to the yard.

Schmidt. I have no bustiness in ter yard.

Soberly. Come, sir, give me the satisfaction I demand. I leave for New York to-morrow.

Schmidt. [*Jumps out of bed, and comes down.*] You go to Nie Yorcke? So have I. I will go mit you.

Soberly. No, sir. You must fight.

Schmidt. No, I'll be shoot if I do.

Soberly. Take your choice, and I'll blow your brains out.

Schmidt. But I don't want mine brains blow out.

Soberly. Now, sir, [*forcing him to take pistol,*] when I count five, fire. One,—

[*Schmidt fires pistol, and exclaims,* "Help, murder." *Noise without.*

Soberly. Ah! you've alarmed the house. I'll meet you in the stage, and shoot you as you go to New York. [*Exit,* L.

Schmidt. Mine Cot in Hemmel! te peoples ish coming. I shall pe kill. [*Looks around, discovers chimney*]. Here ish goot place to hide, I shall pe chimney sweepen. [*Goes up chimney.*

Enter TEDDY, *with pitchfork,* MR. *and* MRS. PLENTIFUL *with candle,* PERSEVERANCE, *with broom, servants, with sticks, &c.*

Teddy. Wait a while, Missus, I'll find him. [*Looks around, at last discovers chimney, shoves pitchfork up chimney.*]

Schmidt. Oh! oh!—murder. [*Exeunt, running* L. *stage dark,*] Oh, I am a persecuted Dutchman. Mine Cot in Hemmel! Tey have come again. Here I will hide. [*Gets into hogshead. Enter* TEDDY *&c., cautiously. Goes to hogshead.*

Teddy. Here he is, Master. I've got the robber. [*Lifts hogshead, Schmidt crawls out. Teddy takes him by ear, and brings him down, covered with soot, &c.*]

Enter CAPTAIN.

Capt. Where is he? Ha—ha! Now, sir, are you not the rascally villain that robbed me of my daughter?

Schmidt. Nien.

Mrs. P. Didn't you get into my bed with your boots on?

Schmidt. Nien. Landlady—two cents change!

Teddy. Didn't ye want to chate me out of my parquisites?

Schmidt. Nien, nien!

Capt. Is not your name Brown, sir?

Schmidt. Nien! I am bad luck Dutchman. To original John Schmidt.

Enter ARABELLA *and* SOBERLY. L. H.

Capt. Arabella, is not this the rascally Brown or Clearstarch?

Ara. La, papa! that's not Gussy.

Schmidt. Nien. I tell him I am te original John Schmidt.

Capt. My dear sir, I ask pardon for all the wrongs I've done you. I thought you Brown.

Schmidt. You make me black and blue. I forgive you, so I get mine garpet pag, un nunder tings, un I come to Nie Yorcke. I shall mit mineself never collect again, py tam.

Soberly. And me, sir. Forgive me and I will be good for all losses, and stand your expenses to New York, where we will be happy to see you at our wedding dinner.

Capt. Yes, Mr. Smith; and old Captain Blowhard will make you welcome.

Schmidt. I don't care. I will vorget un vorgive, un will come von top your house, von te wedding dinner, if you will let me invite mine friends.

Capt. Where are they ?

Schmidt. [*pointing to audience.*] There !

Capt. I never thought of them. Invite them by all means. It would be a dull dinner without their smiling faces.

Schmidt. I will. [*Goes down to audience.*

Ladies un shentlemen,
Mine trouble now, mit me have end,
Mit what I've done and try to do,
I hope mine friends have all please you !
I have suffer much, 'tis gospel true,
But what is dat when I like you ?
Moch more I suffer, and mit cause
To deserve, mine friends, your kind applause !

THE END.

www.ingramcontent.com/pod-product-compliance
Lightning Source LLC
LaVergne TN
LVHW010834120826
845149LV00016B/1370
* 9 7 8 1 4 1 8 1 9 0 6 4 4 *